DK

SUPER SCIENCE LAB

ACTIVITY BOOK

DK

LONDON, NEW YORK,
MELBOURNE, MUNICH, and DELHI

Designed by Jess Bentall
Design assistant Lauren Rosier
Edited by Penny Smith, Alexander Cox, and Lisa Magloff
Science consultants Francis Bate and Donald Franceschetti
Photography Andy Crawford and Guy Archard
Production editor Clare McLean
Jacket editor Mariza O'Keeffe
US editor Margaret Parrish
Publishing manager Bridget Giles

First published in the United States in 2009 by DK Publishing,
375 Hudson Street, New York, New York 10014

Text © 2009 Richard Hammond & September Films Limited,
a division of DCD Media
Layout and design © 2009 Dorling Kindersley Limited

09 10 11 12 13 10 9 8 7 6 5 4 3 2 1
175735—07/09

A catalog record for this book is available from the Library of Congress.

ISBN: 978-0-7566-5550-1

Printed and bound in China by L Rex Printing Co. Ltd

Discover more at

www.dk.com

Picture Credits: The publisher would like to thank the following for their kind
permission to reproduce their photographs: (Key: a-above; b-below/bottom; c-center;
l-left; r-right; t-top) **Walt Anthony:** 23bl, 59cr. **ebog:** Adobe 21br. **Getty Images:** The
Bridgeman Art Library / George Pierre Seurat 20br; Michael Urban / AFP 59cl, 22bl.
iStockphoto.com: Ivar Teunissen 61cla; mammamaart 63fclb. **Photo Scala, Florence:**
Philadelphia Museum of Art 20cr. **Robert Swirsky:** 17t.
All other images © Dorling Kindersley.
For further information see:
www.dkimages.com

Contents

Rockets & Racers

Brain Busters

Body Bits

Secret Agent

Stickers

Balloon Hovercraft

AIR CAN BE USED TO POWER a mini-hovercraft that floats and GLIDES above the ground. Here's how to make one!

On the water

A hovercraft works best on a smooth surface, where there is LESS FRICTION to slow it down. Large hovercrafts are often used on water as ferries or boats. The world speed record for a large hovercraft is 85.75 mph (137.4 km/h).

How does it work?

A hovercraft BLOWS air under itself, making a kind of air cushion. This cushion has enough pressure to support the weight of the craft and any passengers.

In a large hovercraft, a fan blows air under the hovercraft's platform, and the AIR IS TRAPPED between the platform and the ground by a piece of material called the skirt. A small amount of air leaks out from under the skirt, creating the cushion of air.

HOW TO MAKE A HOVERCRAFT

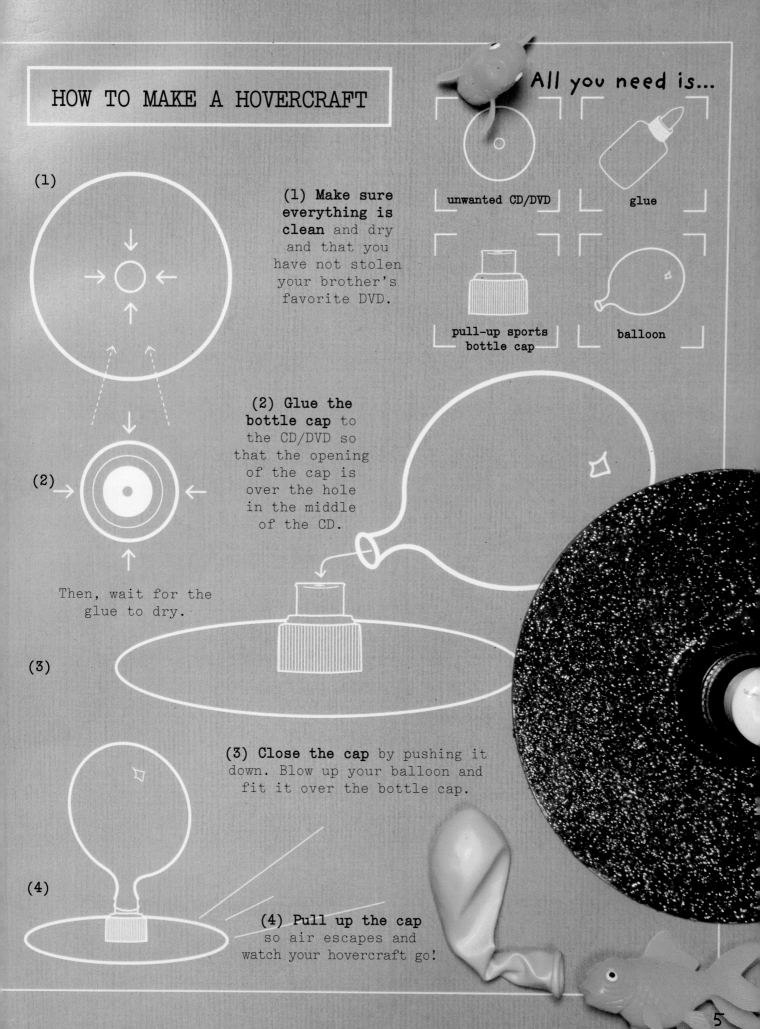

All you need is...

unwanted CD/DVD

glue

pull-up sports bottle cap

balloon

(1)

(1) Make sure everything is clean and dry and that you have not stolen your brother's favorite DVD.

(2)

(2) Glue the bottle cap to the CD/DVD so that the opening of the cap is over the hole in the middle of the CD.

Then, wait for the glue to dry.

(3)

(3) Close the cap by pushing it down. Blow up your balloon and fit it over the bottle cap.

(4)

(4) Pull up the cap so air escapes and watch your hovercraft go!

Racing Spool

With a rubber band as a POWER SOURCE, you can turn a spool of thread into a racer that zooms along at TOP SPEED!

How does it work?

When you twist the rubber band on a racing spool, you STRETCH THE BAND, which stores energy to do work at some future time. This is called potential energy.

The more you twist the rubber band, the more POTENTIAL ENERGY it has. As the rubber band unwinds, the potential energy changes into moving, or kinetic, energy, making the spool turn and move forward.

Rubber-band energy

Here's something to try: make a rubber-band-powered car! You'll need a lightweight material (such as cardboard) for the car's body, and SPOOLS FOR WHEELS. And you'll need a really large rubber band to power the car. Experiment and see what happens.

HOW TO MAKE THE RACER

All you need is...

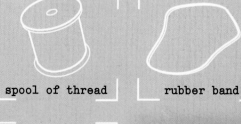

spool of thread

rubber band

wooden skewers

(1) Slip the rubber band through the center of the spool.

(1)

(2) Put a wooden skewer through one loop of the rubber band. Tape it in place. Break off the ends so they don't stick out.

(2)

(3) Push another skewer through the other end of the rubber band. Break it off so one end is flush with the edge of the spool and the other sticks out.

(3)

Wind the long skewer a few times and put the spool on the table. Let it go and... zoom! Off it races.

Boomerang

It spins as it FLIES. But will it come back to you? Make one and see.

MAKE A SPINNING CROSS

All you need is...

cardboard

scissors

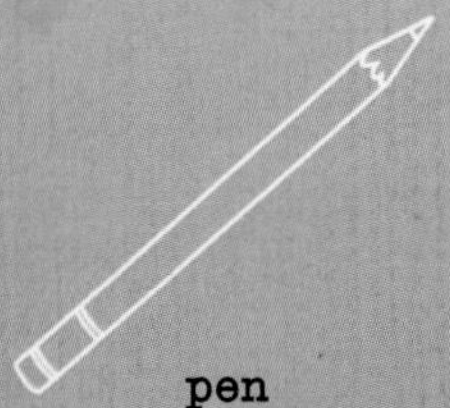

pen

(1) Draw a shape like two adhesive bandages overlapping in a cross.

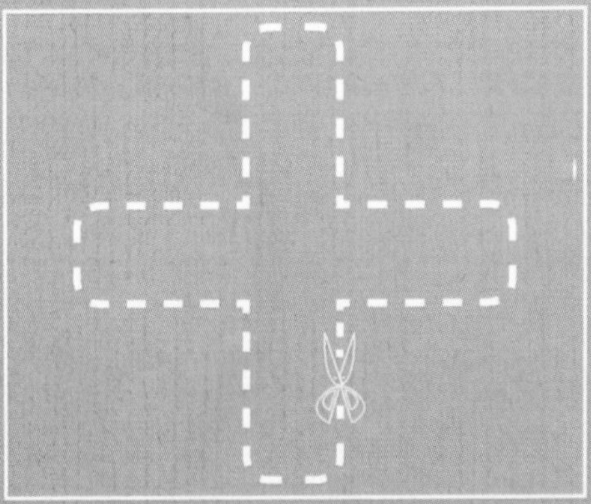

(2) Cut out the boomerang, and slightly bend all four arms upward.

Now launch your boomerang!

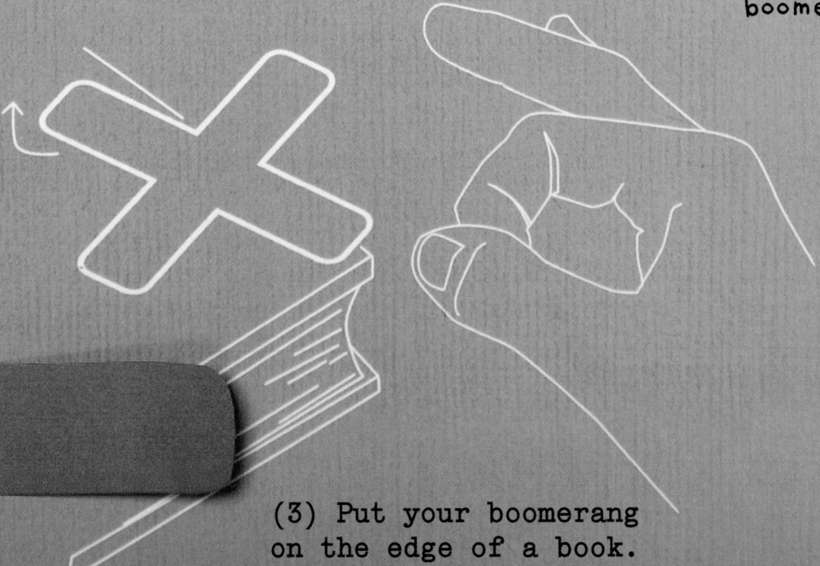

(3) Put your boomerang on the edge of a book. Then flick the boomerang with your finger so that it spins into the air.

You can make this Flying "L" BOOMERANG from cardboard or an expired credit card (but ask Mom or Dad first!).

MAKE A FLYING "L"

All you need is...

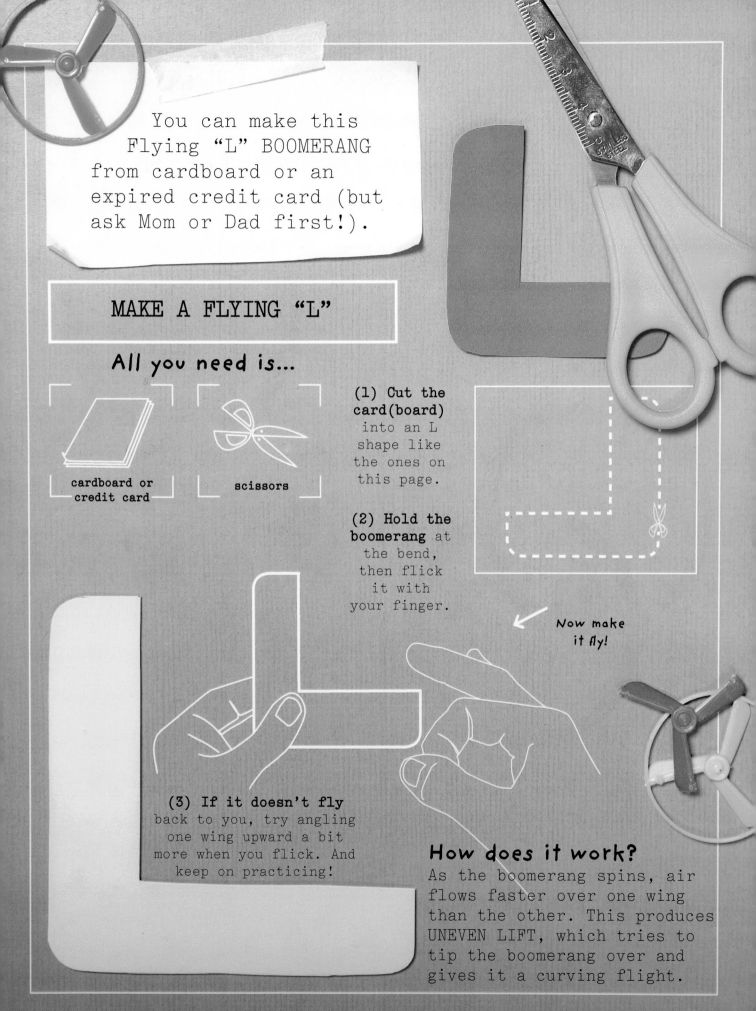

cardboard or credit card

scissors

(1) Cut the card(board) into an L shape like the ones on this page.

(2) Hold the boomerang at the bend, then flick it with your finger.

Now make it fly!

(3) If it doesn't fly back to you, try angling one wing upward a bit more when you flick. And keep on practicing!

How does it work?

As the boomerang spins, air flows faster over one wing than the other. This produces UNEVEN LIFT, which tries to tip the boomerang over and gives it a curving flight.

Flying Crown

IT LOOKS MORE LIKE A HAT than a plane, but this flying crown is king of paper gliders. You might need a little practice... then you can make it fly a really long way!

How does it work?

As the crown moves through the air its top surface ACTS LIKE A WING. Some of its forward movement is turned into lift—a force that pushes the plane upward.

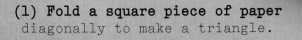

On the fly

The curve of the crown is the same kind of shape as a paraglider's wing. And paragliders are EXCELLENT at flying— they can travel as far as 100 miles (160 km) without an engine.

(1) Fold a square piece of paper diagonally to make a triangle.

(2) and (3) Now fold over the longest edge by about ½ in (1 cm). Fold it over 3 more times.

(4) Twist around the long edge to make a circle. Make sure the folded part is on the inside of the circle.

(5) Join the circle together by pushing one end of the folded edge inside the other.

(6) Roll the point of the crown around a pencil, then unwind it so that it curls outward. Cut a slit 1 in (2 cm) long into the curled point.

(7) Now throw your plane—hold it so the thin part of the circle faces downward, and the point is to the back.

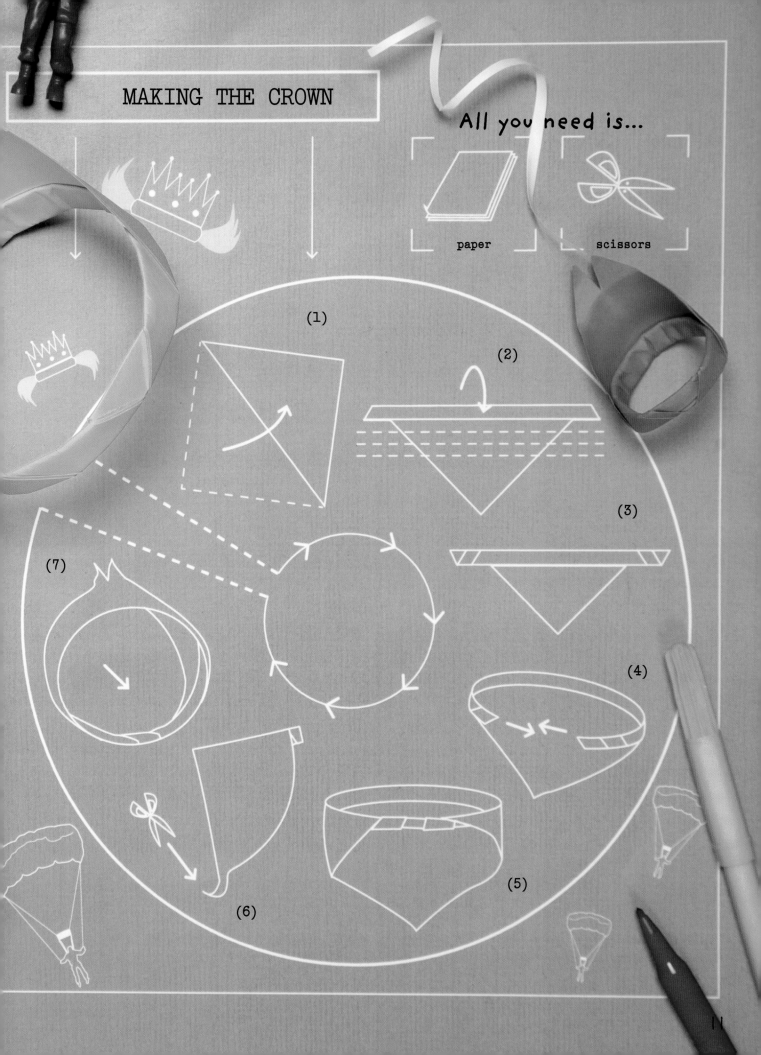

MAKING THE CROWN

Cone Rocket

THREE, TWO, ONE, BLAST OFF!
Here's how to make your own
rocket—and launch it using a
clever trick with air pressure.

All you need is...

paper

scissors

tape

wooden skewers
(points broken off)

straw

plastic bottle

modeling
clay

HOW TO MAKE A ROCKET

(1)

(1) Draw a half circle on paper.

(2) Cut it out.
Then twist it around
into a cone shape
(leaving a teeny
hole at the tip).
Tape it together.

(2)

(3)

(3) Push the skewer through the hole and
secure with modeling clay.
Now decorate your cone.

(4) Put the straw into the plastic bottle so it sticks out 3 in (8 cm) or
so. Secure with modeling clay, making
sure the opening is sealed.

(4)

(5)

(5) Slide the wooden skewer into the straw in the bottle. Squeeze
the bottle firmly...

How does it work?

Even though you can't see air, you know it's there. Although air molecules are INVISIBLE, they still have mass and take up space—this means air has PUSHING POWER. In this rocket, the straw is the only way for air in the bottle to get out. When you squeeze the bottle, more pressure is put on the air inside. The air is forced out through the straw, making the rocket take off.

Are you under pressure?

The air in Earth's atmosphere is PRESSING against every little bit of you with a force of 15 lbs per square inch (1 kg per square centimeter). So why doesn't it squash you? Remember that you have air inside you, too, and that air BALANCES OUT the pressure outside so you stay firm and not all squishy.

ZzApP!

WhoOSh!

... and WATCH
THE ROCKET FLY!

cRAsH!

13

Moving Pictures

WHEN YOU WATCH A FILM, you're looking at a moving image, right? WRONG! What you're actually seeing are lots of still pictures one after another.

The images change so quickly that your brain is tricked into thinking you're seeing a moving picture.

MAKE A MOVING-IMAGE FLICK BOOK

Find a pad of paper with at least 20 pages in it.

Draw a picture on the last page. Trace it onto the previous page, with a few small changes (or use the stickers on pages 54 and 59).

Keep tracing from page to page until you've made a kind of cartoon story. Flick through the pages and your cartoon will look like it's moving!

At the movies

The films you see at the movie theater are made up of thousands of pictures joined together in long strips. These strips are wound up on FILM REELS. If you unwind a whole movie it will probably be more than 2 miles (3 km) long.

PICTURE SPINNER

All you need is...

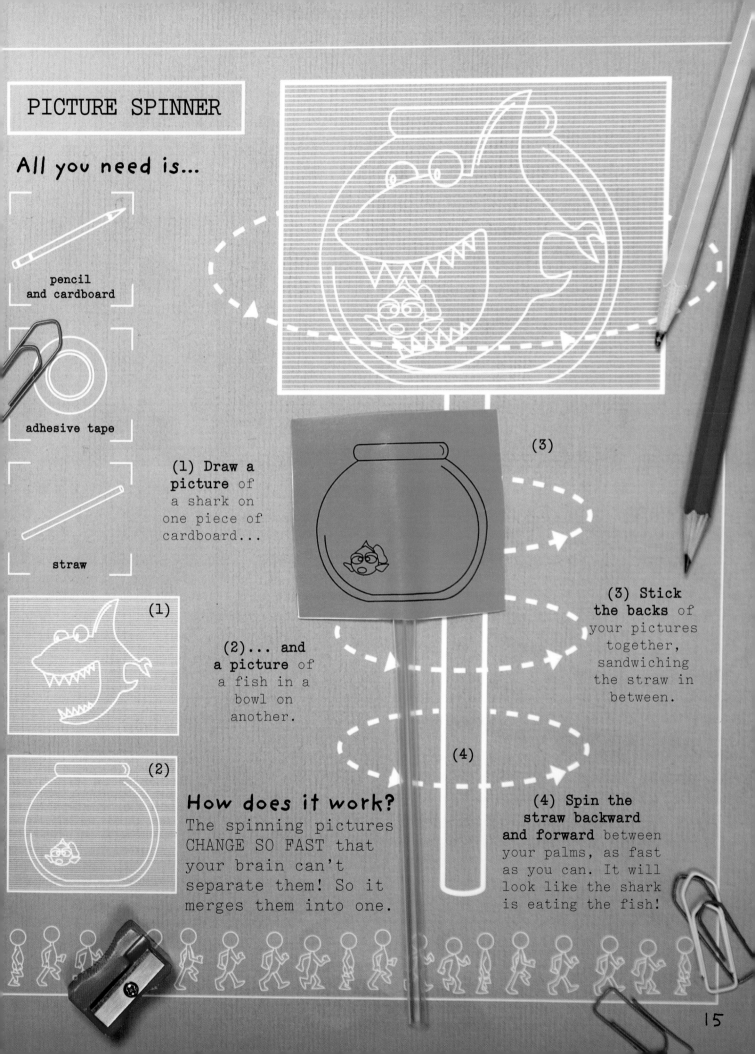

pencil
and cardboard

adhesive tape

straw

(1)

(2)

(1) Draw a picture of a shark on one piece of cardboard...

(2)... and a picture of a fish in a bowl on another.

(3)

(4)

(3) Stick the backs of your pictures together, sandwiching the straw in between.

(4) Spin the straw backward and forward between your palms, as fast as you can. It will look like the shark is eating the fish!

How does it work?
The spinning pictures CHANGE SO FAST that your brain can't separate them! So it merges them into one.

Seeing in 3-D

These glasses use the fact that you have TWO EYES to make pictures jump off the page. Try them out on these pictures.

HOW TO MAKE 3-D GLASSES

All you need is...

cardboard

scissors

red and blue acetate

glue

(1) Cut out two rectangles of cardboard big enough to cover your eyes. Glue them together around three edges, leaving one long edge open.

(2) Cut out two square eyeholes and a nose hole.

(3) Cut out two acetate squares, one red and one blue, big enough to cover the eyeholes.

(4) Slide the acetate between the cardboard rectangles and glue in place—make sure the red square will cover your left eye.

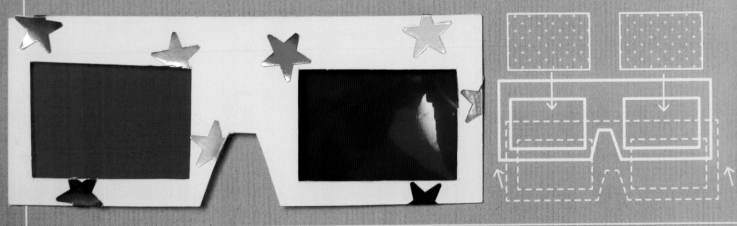

3-D IMAGE MAKER

All you need is...

tracing paper

red and blue markers

(1) Draw a simple picture in red marker on a piece of tracing paper.

(2) On another piece, trace your image in blue. Put the red image on the blue one.

How does it work?

When you look at the image above through 3-D glasses, each eye sees a slightly different picture, just like when you're looking at a scene in the real world. This fools your brain into thinking the image is 3-D.

(3) Look at them with your glasses. Can you see a 3-D image?

Möbius Magic

Want to make some SURPRISING SHAPES? Then twist a strip of paper and see what happens!

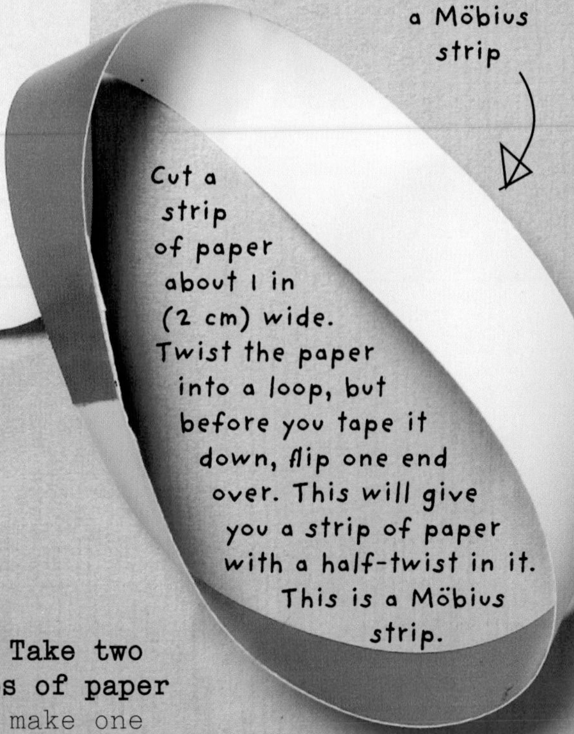

How to make a Möbius strip

Cut a strip of paper about 1 in (2 cm) wide. Twist the paper into a loop, but before you tape it down, flip one end over. This will give you a strip of paper with a half-twist in it. This is a Möbius strip.

MAKE A MÖBIUS SQUARE

All you need is...

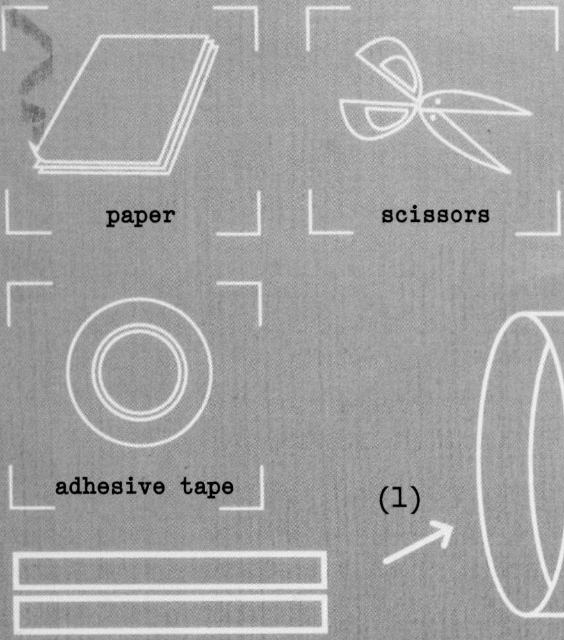

paper

scissors

adhesive tape

(1) Take two strips of paper and make one Möbius strip and one normal loop (no twists).

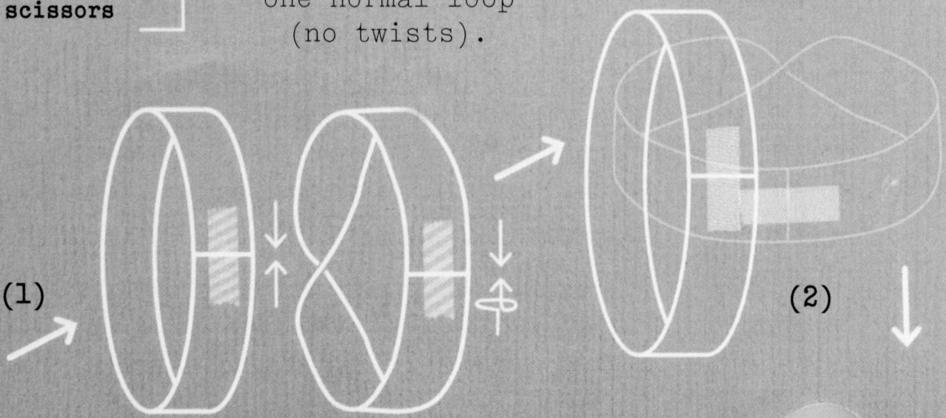

(1)

(2)

(2) Tape them together at right angles to each other.

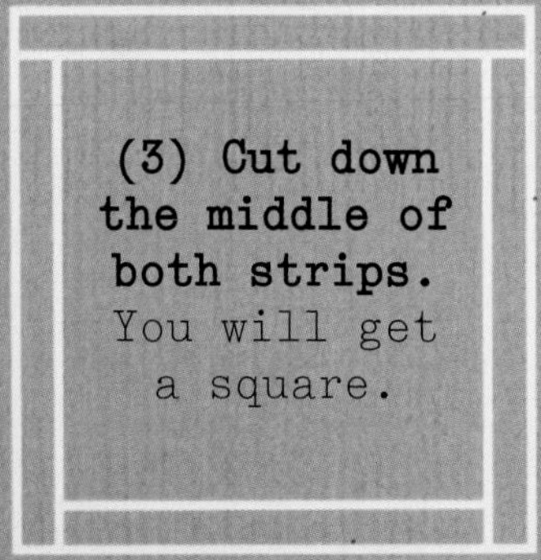

(3) Cut down the middle of both strips. You will get a square.

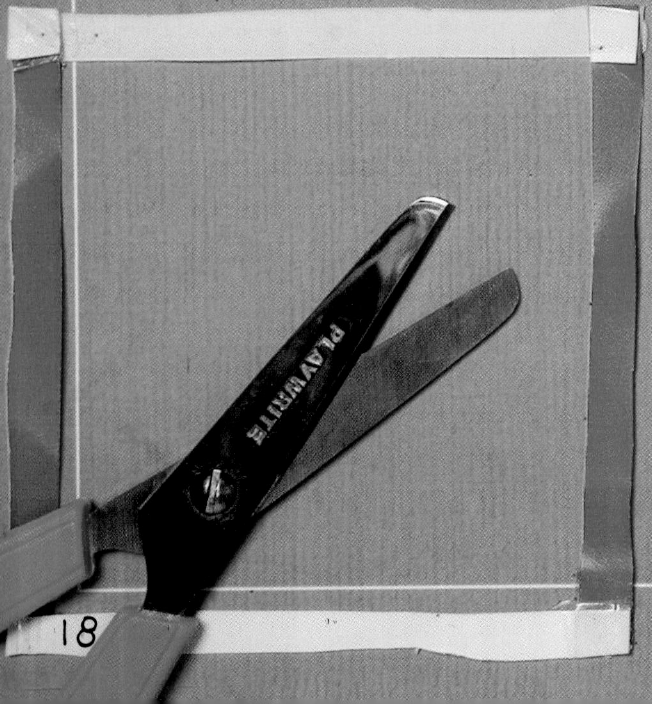

(3)

How does it work?

The Möbius strip only has ONE SIDE and ONE EDGE. If you draw a line down the middle of the strip until you get back to your starting point, you will find that you draw on BOTH SIDES OF THE PAPER without lifting your pen. The twist in the paper makes you change sides as you draw.

MAKE LINKED MÖBIUS HEARTS

All you need is...

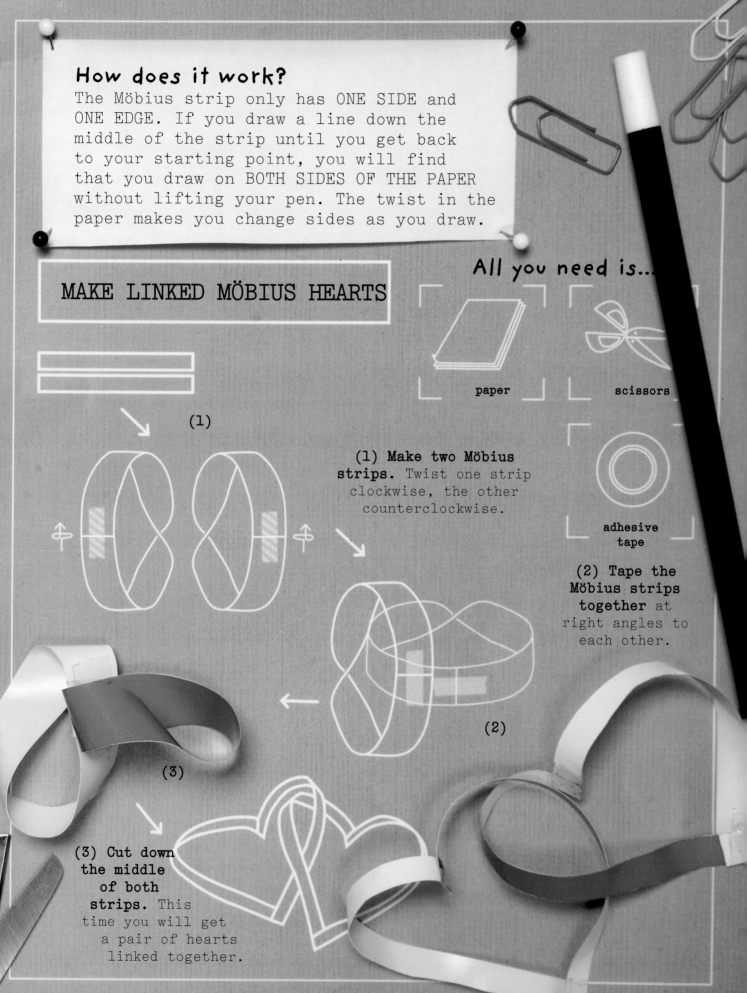

paper

scissors

adhesive tape

(1)

(1) Make two Möbius strips. Twist one strip clockwise, the other counterclockwise.

(2) Tape the Möbius strips together at right angles to each other.

(2)

(3)

(3) Cut down the middle of both strips. This time you will get a pair of hearts linked together.

Pixel Power

Some pictures are made up of lots of TINY DOTS CALLED PIXELS. When you stand back, the dots seem to MERGE together to make a big image. That's PIXEL POWER!

How does it work?

The screen of a COMPUTER MONITOR or television contains many tiny pixels. Because the pixels are so small, when we stand farther away we see solid images. When different colored pixels are placed next to each other, their colors SEEM TO BLEND together. So a green dot and a red dot next to each other seem to be yellow.

Pixel Art

Painter Georges Seurat (1859-1891) created a type of painting style called pointillism. Instead of painting in brush strokes, he used tiny dots of color. When you look at one of his paintings, your eyes blend the dots together.

HOW TO MAKE PIXEL ART

All you need is...

pixel stickers

graph paper

markers

(1) First draw a fairly simple picture on the grid here.

(2) Use the small square stickers from the sticker sheet to color in your image.

(3) You can also make pixel art on graph paper. Draw your outline, then color in your picture by filling in the squares with colored markers, one color per square.

Pixels are popular! Artist Chuck Close turns photos of his friends and family into large-scale grid pictures (center left). And a creative team called eBoy makes pixel art on computers (right).

Optical Illusions

Sometimes your brain has difficulty MAKING SENSE of what your eyes see. So what does it think of the OPTICAL ILLUSIONS on this page?

At first glance, these triangles look like regular **3-D shapes.** But are they?

THE BOX TRICK

What are these?

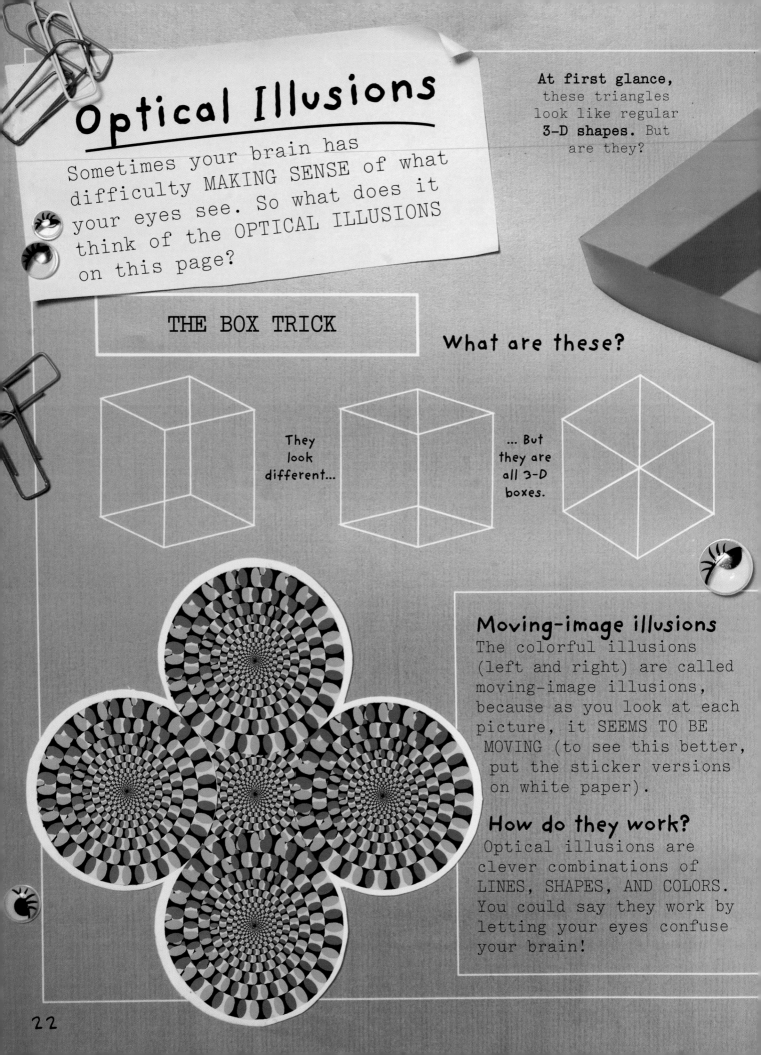

They look different...

... But they are all 3-D boxes.

Moving-image illusions

The colorful illusions (left and right) are called moving-image illusions, because as you look at each picture, it SEEMS TO BE MOVING (to see this better, put the sticker versions on white paper).

How do they work?

Optical illusions are clever combinations of LINES, SHAPES, AND COLORS. You could say they work by letting your eyes confuse your brain!

This is an impossible triangle, also called a Penrose triangle. Its sides look as if they move away and toward you at the same time.

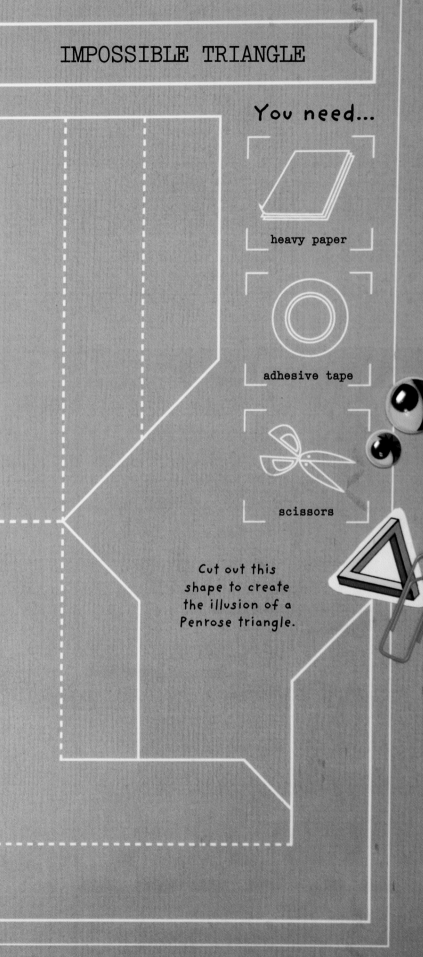

You need...

heavy paper

adhesive tape

scissors

Cut out this shape to create the illusion of a Penrose triangle.

MAKE A PENROSE TRIANGLE

1. First photocopy or trace the pattern onto a sheet of heavy paper and cut it out.

2. Fold along the dotted lines. You should end up with a shape that looks a little like an L, with one extra leg sticking out.

3. Put this shape on a table and move around it until it looks like a Penrose triangle.

23

Rockets & Racers Quiz

1. All the animals here have been sent into space. But which went first?

Cricket, mice, rats, frogs, newts, fruit flies, squirrel, snail, carp, monkey, dog, silkworms, toadfish, sea urchin, swordtail fish...

2. What's the world record for the flight of a paper airplane?

a. 20 ft (6 m)
b. 54 ft (16.5 m)
c. 112 ft (34.14 m)
d. 20 miles (32 km)

3. What is the land speed record for a wheeled vehicle?

a. 127 mph (205 km/h)
b. 351 mph (565 km/h)
c. 600 mph (970 km/h)
d. 763 mph (1,228 km/h)

4. The oldest known boomerang is from which country?

a. Australia
b. Poland
c. India
d. China

FORMULA

ANSWERS: **(1)** Fruit flies were first, launched aboard a V2 rocket in 1947. **(2)** c—In 2007 Lucas Tortora set the record for distance and hang time of a paper airplane. His plane stayed up for 83 seconds. **(3)** d—763 mph (1,228 km/h). Answer "a" is the fastest steam-powered vehicle, answer "b" is the fastest motorcycle speed, and answer "c" is the speed of the first wheeled vehicle to break the sound barrier. **(4)** b—The oldest known boomerang was discovered in a cave in Poland. It was made of mammoth's tusk and is believed to be about 30,000 years old.

Brain Busters Quiz

1. 3-D glasses work because of the distance between your pupils. Everyone's pupils are about the same distance apart. What's this distance?

    a. 1 in (2.5 cm)
    b. 2 in (5 cm)
    c. 3 in (7.5 cm)
    d. 4 in (10 cm)

2. When you look at a TV you see an image made up of pixels. About how many pixels are on an average 24 in (61 cm) TV screen?

    a. 500
    b. 1,200
    c. 480,000
    d. 1,200,000

3. The picture spinner (on page 15) was invented in 1824 by Dr. Mark Roget. What was it first used for?

    a. a toy
    b. scientific research
    c. an early type of movie
    d. an unusual type of book

4. Optical illusions are designed to confuse your brain—something that can be put to practical use. Which one of the following does not use optical illusion?

    a. art
    b. architecture
    c. cooking
    d. stick insects

ANSWERS: **(1)** b—Human pupils are about 2 in (5 cm) apart. **(2)** c—There are about 480,000 pixels on a normal TV. High-definition TVs have as many as 30 million pixels. **(3)** b—Called a thaumatrope, it was used in scientific research to prove something called persistence of vision. This is the way your brain sees fast-moving images as if they were overlapping. The thaumatrope was also used as a toy and is the first type of animated movie. **(4)** c—Art and architecture use perspective, and stick insects use camouflage. These are types of optical illusion.

Nose Your Flavors

YOU TASTE with your tongue—everyone knows that. But do you also sense flavors with your nose? Here's a little game that puts TASTE to the TEST.

A FEAST FOR THE SENSES
This test works best when you use chips of the same size and texture. The way food looks, feels, and even sounds has a big impact on our sense of taste.

HOW TO TEST TASTE

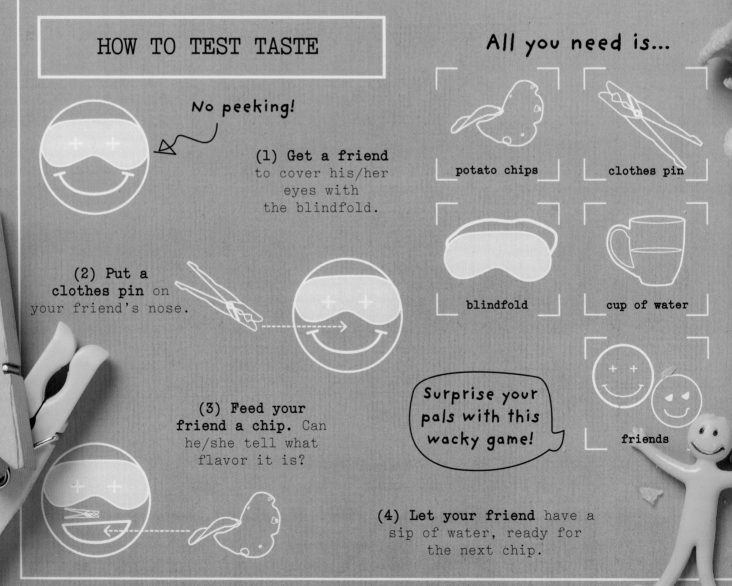

No peeking!

(1) **Get a friend** to cover his/her eyes with the blindfold.

(2) **Put a clothes pin** on your friend's nose.

(3) **Feed your friend a chip.** Can he/she tell what flavor it is?

(4) **Let your friend** have a sip of water, ready for the next chip.

All you need is...

potato chips

clothes pin

blindfold

cup of water

friends

Surprise your pals with this wacky game!

(5) Now, give your friend a different flavored chip. Can he/she tell what flavor it is this time?

(6) Keep going with different chips. Remember to keep score. A correct flavor gets one point! Run out of flavors? Well, now it's your turn. Can you beat your friend's score?

Choose just one shape of chip, or they'll guess the flavor from the texture.

What's happening?

The TASTE BUDS on your tongue can only sense five basic flavors: sweet, salty, bitter, sour, and umami (a meaty flavor).

About 70 percent of what you "taste" is actually SMELLED. Food smells drift into your nose through passages at the back of your mouth. When you pin your nose, you are blocking off your sense of SMELL. This makes it hard to tell the difference between flavors.

YUM YUM!

Toothpaste Taste

After eating you should always BRUSH YOUR TEETH. Here's a teeth-brushing experiment. After the chip test brush your teeth and then try drinking some ORANGE JUICE. What happens?

WHY DOES IT TASTE SO DISGUSTING? Well, to be honest, scientists aren't totally sure. One opinion is that an ingredient in toothpaste, which makes it foamy, dulls the SWEETNESS DETECTORS in your taste buds. This gives the orange juice a BITTER flavor. Yuck!

Sick Trick

This pretend vomit is perfect for a PRACTICAL JOKE! You can even gross out your friends and family by eating it. But don't blame us if it tastes a bit weird...

Don't eat your trick vomit if it gets dirty. Keep it in the fridge until it's time for your practical joke.

The art of a good practical joke is to make sure the person you play it on will also find it funny...

Why do we throw up?

The digestive system is very vulnerable to attack because it is where your body absorbs most of the nutrients you need to grow, repair, and energize.

Vomiting is actually one of the digestive system's main defense mechanisms. The body rejects food when you feel unwell or if you eat something that might hurt you.

WHAT MAKES US SICK?
Your digestive system protects itself from danger by emptying the stomach. Vomit is just partially digested food.

Real vomit is very acidic, because it contains gastric acid from your stomach. This acid is strong enough to kill germs, and can even dissolve an iron nail!

HOW TO MAKE EDIBLE VOMIT

All you need is...

apple sauce

carrot

sweet corn

plate

cocoa powder

gelatin

cup

teaspoon

tablespoon

knife

spatula

(1) Scoop three tablespoons of apple sauce into the cup. Add one teaspoon of cocoa powder.

(2) Chop the carrot into little cubes, and drain the sweet corn.

(3) Add some pieces of carrot and sweet corn to the apple sauce. Stir in three teaspoons of gelatin.

(4) Spoon the mixture onto a plate and mold into a splat shape.

(5) Leave it in the fridge overnight to set. Then use the spatula to place it on a clean surface. Don't put it on the floor!

Crazy Crackers

WHEN YOU SWALLOW, food falls down into your BELLY, doesn't it? Here's an experiment that tests how food travels through you.

HOW TO EAT UPSIDE DOWN

*WARNING!

Eating upside down is perfectly safe—but make sure you have a friend around, just in case you get the giggles and food goes down the wrong way.

All you need is...

cushion

crackers

a wall

mouth

head

(1) Take the **cushion** and place it on the floor next to the wall.

(2) Place your **head on the cushion** and do a headstand. You can lean against the wall for stability.

(3) Now eat the **cracker,** a little piece at a time.

(4) **Can you eat it?** What happens when you swallow?

How does it work?

Your digestive system doesn't need gravity to move food through your body. Muscles push the chewed food into your stomach and through your intestines.

Balls 'n' Tights

YOU ALREADY KNOW your body uses muscle power to push food along. But how does this work?

What's happening?

The balls in this game represent the food in your belly. As you squeeze, your hands act like the rings of muscle pushing food along. The muscles tighten in waves to keep food moving in one direction.

MAKING BALLS 'N' TIGHTS

(1) Cut the tights in half, so you have two single legs...

...then cut off the toes.

All you need is...

old tights

tennis balls

two chairs

scissors

(2) Tie one end of each leg to the first chair. Then put a ball in the open end of each leg and tie the other end to the second chair.

(3) Slide the chairs apart until the tights are taut.

(4) Game on! First person to push their ball from one end to the other wins!

Snip, snip!

Breathing Bottle

What can a PLASTIC BOTTLE tell us about the way we breathe? A surprising amount, actually. It all has to do with AIR PRESSURE.

UNDER PRESSURE
Air pressure is the pushing force of air against other materials. When a lot of air is forced into a small area—like when you're blowing up a balloon—this increases the air pressure.

I'M FULL OF HOT AIR!

This bottle helps explain air pressure and its role in helping us breathe. Gas moves from areas of higher air pressure to areas of lower air pressure.

What's happening?

The balloon acts like the muscle below your lungs, called the diaphragm. As the balloon expands, it increases air pressure in the bottle, pushing air out of the small hole. As the balloon deflates, the air pressure drops and air enters through the hole. Something similar happens in your lungs. As the diaphragm lengthens, it increases the air pressure in your lungs, making you breathe out. When the diaphragm shortens, it lowers the air pressure, drawing air in.

MAKE A BREATHING BOTTLE

All you need is...

balloon

bottle

pencil

a friend

(1) Remove the lid from the bottle— you don't need it.

(2) Use the pencil to make a small hole 2 in (5 cm) from the bottle's base.

(3) Keep hold of the balloon and carefully feed it into the bottle.

(4) With the balloon still inside the bottle, stretch the mouth of the balloon over the opening of the bottle.

(5) Try blowing up the balloon first with, then without, your finger over the hole. It won't inflate if you have your finger over the hole!

(6) Here's a good trick. Show your friend how easy it is to blow up the balloon. Remember to keep the hole uncovered.

TRY HARDER!

(7) Then ask your friend to try—but "help" them hold the bottle, and secretly cover up the hole.

Your friend won't be able to blow the balloon up!

Farting Fun

Surely, there's NO REAL SCIENCE in farting? In fact, there's plenty—just try these experiments.

MAKING A FART WHISTLE

Whoopee Cushion

When anyone sits down it emits a REAL Bronx Cheer

DO NOT INFLATE TOO HEAVILY

MADE IN CHINA

The fart whistle works in the same way as a whoopee cushion.

All you need is...

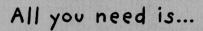

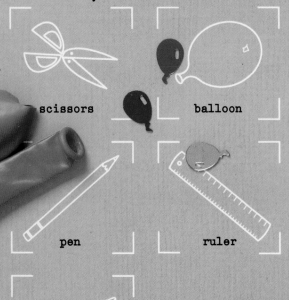

scissors

balloon

pen

ruler

mouth

(1) **Lay the balloon flat,** and measure about 4 in (10 cm) up from the mouth of the balloon.

(2) **Draw a line and carefully cut along it.** The balloon should now be funnel-shaped.

(3) **Now blow into the balloon whistle**—it will make a noise just like a real fart!

Parp!

Rasp!

Fart!

MAKING FART GOO

(1) **Put 1 teaspoon of craft glue** into the bowl and mix in a few drops of food coloring.

(2) **Spray some starch into the teaspoon,** and stir it into the glue.

(3) **After four teaspoons of starch** you should get a sticky goo.

(4) **Pour the goo into the small jar.** Then pop it in the fridge for 30 minutes.

Toot!

Honk!

(5) **Move your finger in and out of the goo.** The trapped air will make a farting noise!

small jar

craft glue

food coloring

bowl

teaspoon

spray starch

What's happening?

Farts are caused by the buildup of gas in your intestines. The gas mostly comes from the chemical reactions that break down food. This gas is pushed through your intestines during digestion, and comes out of your bottom.

The fart noise depends on a muscle in your bottom called the sphincter—the faster the gas exits and the tighter the muscle, the louder the noise.

Eye See You

AS A SECRET AGENT, you'll need to keep an eye on the enemy, using clever GADGETS. Fear not—here's how to make your own SPY-EYE PERISCOPE.

Can you see around corners?

Periscopes help you see above high obstacles like fences and walls. You can even use them sideways and peer around corners!

Spy science explained!

LIGHT RAYS always travel in straight lines. Mirrored surfaces, like the pieces of cardboard in our periscope, bounce light rays back out at EXACTLY THE SAME ANGLE that they arrive, so that you see a reflection.

The mirrors in the periscope are angled at 45 degrees, which is the perfect angle to bounce light from one mirror onto the other, and then into your eye.

Sneaky sight

Periscopes are used by submarines to look above the waves without giving away their position to enemy ships. The first periscope was used on a submarine in 1902.

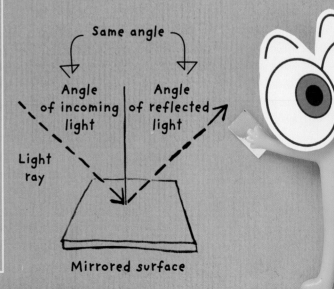

Same angle

Angle of incoming light

Angle of reflected light

Light ray

Mirrored surface

HOW TO MAKE A PERISCOPE

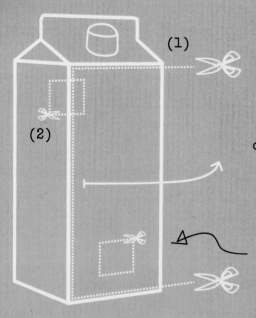

(1)

(2)

All you need is...

juice carton

mirrored cardboard

tape

scissors

(1) Cut along three sides of the carton to open it up.

(2) At the top of one side, cut an eye-sized hole. This is the viewhole.

Then cut another hole at the bottom of the opposite side. This is the eyehole.

(3)

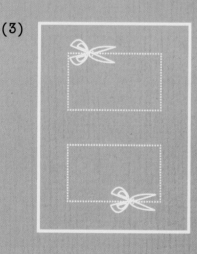

(3) Cut two rectangles of mirrored cardboard. Don't cut them too small.

(4) Place a rectangle of mirrored cardboard into the bottom of the carton at a 45 degree angle and do the same for the mirrored cardboard at the top of the carton.

(4)

Tape both pieces of cardboard in place. The mirrored sides should face each other.

(5) Close up the carton with tape. If your angles are correct, you can look in the eyehole and see out of the viewhole!

(5)

If not, change the angles of the cardboard until you can.

Guilty Pen!

Note: Don't use permanent markers!

SOMETIMES SPIES SEND secret messages to each other. Here's how to find out WHOSE PEN was used to write the secret note.

HOW TO CATCH THE CULPRIT

All you need is...

(1) Ask a friend to secretly write "SECRET..." on a piece of blotting paper with one of the three felt pens. Remember the periods!

(2) Cut three strips of blotting paper, about the depth of the tub.

(3) Take a pen and make a dot near the bottom of each strip. Use a different pen for each.

(4) Cut a strip out of the "SECRET..." note. Use a period as your dot for the test.

plastic tub

blotting paper

3 black felt pens

pitcher of water

friends

string

Evidence strip

Suspect pen strips

paper clips

Use three different makes of felt pen.

(5) Fix some string across the top of the plastic tub—for example, using tape—so it looks like a tightrope. Fill the tub with water to a depth of $^1/_2$ in (1 cm).

(6) Paper clip each strip to the string, so that the very end of the strip (but not the dot) hangs into the water.

Evidence strip

Suspect pen strips

(7) Leave for 10 minutes to allow the blotting paper to absorb water.

Spy science explained!

The ink in black pens is a mixture of different colored chemicals. Some chemicals dissolve easier in water and spread up the blotting paper, creating a unique color pattern.

Your evidence strip is a colorful "pen-print" that you can use to identify the guilty pen!

Now compare the "pen-print" of each suspect strip to the original evidence strip. You should now know which is the guilty pen!

Remember to note down which dot belongs to which pen.

GUILTY!

Finding Prints

A CARELESS CRIMINAL can leave clues at a crime scene. A fingerprint can be a key piece of EVIDENCE— so start dusting!

HOW TO DUST FOR PRINTS

All you need is...

blusher brush

mirror

plate

talcum powder

black cardboard

tape

This one's been dusted already.

(1) Press your finger firmly on the mirror.

(2) Dip the brush in talcum powder, shake off the excess powder, then use the brush to dust the mirror.

Make sure you dust carefully, so you don't smudge the print.

(3) Take a strip of tape, and gently stick it over the white fingerprint. Slowly peel it off.

(4) Stick the tape on the black cardboard. Now you can see the fingerprint in detail!

Making Prints

YOU'VE FOUND FINGERPRINTS. But they are only useful if you can compare them. That means INKY fingers!

There are THREE types of fingerprint.

ARCH   WHORL   LOOP

HOW TO INK PRINTS

All you need is...

ink pad

white cardboard

magnifying glass

(1) **Gently place** the tip of your finger onto the ink pad.

Spy science

Your hands are covered in tiny grooves, which provide friction and help you grip. To add extra grip, skin oils are channeled along the grooves. It's these oils that leave the outline of the fingerprint on shiny surfaces.

(2) **Now gently press your finger** on the white cardboard. Don't smudge it!

We all have unique fingerprints—even identical twins. So fingerprinting is a foolproof way of identifying the culprit!

(3) **Use the magnifying glass** to look at the hoops and loops of the print.

WARNING!
INTRUDER!

Intruder Alert!

AS A SPY, you'll need to keep top-secret files from ENEMY AGENTS. Protect your bedroom with an INTRUDER ALARM!

HOW TO MAKE AN ALARM

All you need is...

scissors

musical card

book

fishing wire

(1) Peel back the piece of cardboard that is hiding all the electrical parts in the musical card.

You can feel where the circuit is in the card.

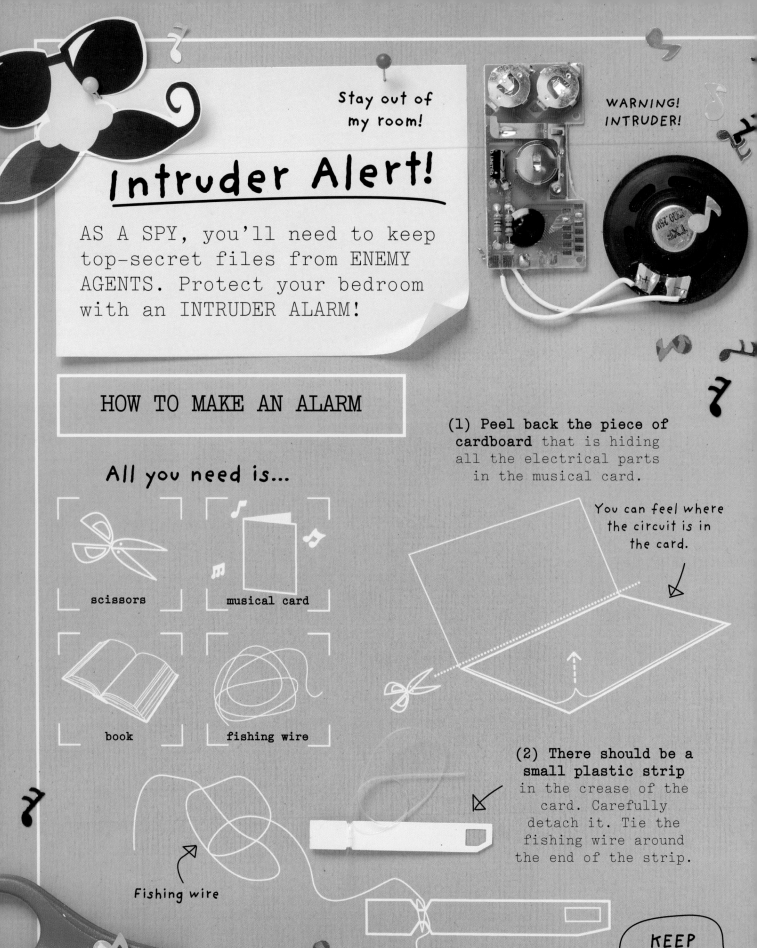

Fishing wire

(2) There should be a small plastic strip in the crease of the card. Carefully detach it. Tie the fishing wire around the end of the strip.

KEEP OUT!

SUPER-SPY TOP TIP
You have to position the intruder alarm just right. Make sure that when the door opens it tugs on the fishing wire and pulls the plastic strip out of the pincer.

Spy science explained!
The mechanism in the card is an electrical circuit connecting a battery to a speaker. When the plastic strip is in the pincer, it stops the flow of electricity, so the buzzer doesn't sound. But when the door opens, it pulls the strip from the pincer, and this completes the electrical circuit. The speaker converts electricity to sound: INTRUDER ALERT!

(3) Cut away the rest of the card so you are left with just the circuit board and speaker.

(4) Attach the loose end of the fishing wire to your bedroom door handle.

(5) Locate the metal pincer on the circuit board.

Pincer

(6) Carefully, hook the hole on the plastic strip under the pincer.

(7) Now hide the circuit board and speaker in a heavy book, and make sure the fishing line is taut. You're ready for any intruders!

DNA Extraction

Spy missions can be challenging. Do you want to SEE WHAT YOU'RE MADE OF? Now you can—let's EXTRACT some DNA.

Your DNA is completely unique to you, unless you're an identical twin.

All you need is...

clean glass

glass of salty water

nail polish remover

dishwashing liquid

pitcher of water

freezer

wooden kebab sticks

You can keep your DNA in a jar or a test tube and show it to your friends!

HOW TO EXTRACT YOUR DNA

(1) **Put the nail polish remover** in the freezer for 10 minutes.

(2) **Take a clean glass** and add three teaspoons of tap water...

... then add one teaspoon of dishwashing liquid.

It tastes pretty disgusting!

(3) Take a mouthful of salty water and swill it around your mouth.

(4) Now, spit the salty water into the glass of dishwashing liquid and water. Swish the mixture around in the glass for five minutes.

A single hair, or a drop of blood or saliva can be used as DNA evidence in an investigation.

(5) Slowly pour some nail polish remover into the glass, so it forms a layer on top.

Spy science explained!

When you swill salty water in your mouth, you're washing tiny cells from your cheeks and gums—and these cells contain DNA.

What is DNA? DNA is the set of genetic instructions that makes you who you are. It is found in every cell of your body.

Everyone's DNA is unique (except for identical twins). Investigators can use DNA evidence from a crime scene to find and convict criminals.

(6) After five minutes, white strands will appear in the layer of nail polish remover. Use the kebab sticks to fish these out—they are made of your DNA!

Body Bits Quiz

1. Food travels a long way through your body. How long are the average adult's intestines in total (large and small together)?

    a. 3 ft (1 m)
    b. 15 ft (5 m)
    c. 32 ft (10 m)
    d. 320 ft (100 m)

2. Smell something bad? If you were a dog it would smell worse, because dogs are more sensitive to odors than humans. But by how much?

    a. 2 times
    b. 10 times
    c. 1,000 times
    d. 10,000 times

3. Farting—everyone does it, even movie stars. But how many times, on average, does a person fart a day?

    a. Never!
    b. Once
    c. 14 times
    d. 14,000 times

4. Eating dinner can take a matter of minutes, especially if it's your favorite meal. But how long, on average, does it take for the food to be digested?

    a. 5 minutes
    b. 1 hour
    c. 24 hours
    d. 80 hours

Fart!

ANSWERS:
(1) c.
Your small intestine is about 26 ft (8 m) long and your large intestine is slightly smaller, only 5 ft (2 m). (2) d. Dogs are very sensitive to smells because they have about 1 billion smell receptors. (3) c. This is an average—some days it will be more, other days fewer. (4) d. 80 hours—that's just over three days!

When anyone sits down it emits a REAL Bronx cheer DO NOT INFLATE TOO HEAVILY

Secret Agent Quiz

1. The code for human DNA consists of four letters—A, C, G, and T. But how many letters long is the human genetic code?

    a. 300 letters
    b. 3,000 letters
    c. 3 million letters
    d. 3 billion letters

2. The curves and creases in a fingerprint are given names relating to their shape. Which of the below is not a type of fingerprint?

    a. Arch
    b. Loop
    c. Hoop
    d. Whorl

3. Night-vision goggles are a must for any spy. But what type of light do they detect to help spies see in the dark?

a. Twilight
  b. Infrared light
    c. Cosmic light
      d. Ultra-blue light

4. During World War II, the Germans developed a code machine called Enigma. It was really hard to crack. How many different ways could each letter in a message be encoded?

    a. 15 billion billion
    b. 15 million
    c. 15,000
    d. 15

ANSWERS: (1) d. 3 billion letters long! **(2)** c. Arch, loop, and whorl are all real fingerprint types. Which do you have? **(3)** b. Humans see within a small range called visible light. Night vision increases what we see into other ranges, including infrared light. **(4)** a. 15,000,000,000,000,000,000. After a few errors from the Germans, it still took the Allies years to crack Enigma (and they used a computer).

47

Stickers

WE HOPE YOU HAVE HAD A BLAST
with all the Super Science
activities. Now, get STUCK
into over 800 fun STICKERS!